NEW WOMEN IN POLITICS

by kathleen bowman

Creative Education

Published by Creative Educational Society, Inc.,
123 South Broad Street, Mankato, Minnesota 56001.
Copyright © 1976 by Creative Educational Society, Inc.
International copyrights reserved in all countries.
No part of this book may be reproduced in any form
without written permission from the publisher
Printed in the United States.

ISBN: 0-87191-507-3
Photo Credits:
UPI: pp. 5, 6, 7, 9, 10, 11, 13, 19, 20, 23, 24, 26, 29, 30, 32, 35, 36, 37, 38, 39, 41, 42, 45, 47
Seafarers Union of North America: pp. 15, 17

Design concept and cover by Larry Soule

Library of Congress Cataloging in Publication Data
Bowman, Kathleen.
New women in politics.
SUMMARY: Brief biographies of Bess Myerson,
Patsy Mink, Dolores Huerta, Yvonne Brathwaite Burke,
Elizabeth Holtzman, Barbara Jordan, and Ella Grosso
—all women involved in politics who are sincerely
dedicated to solving human problems.
1. Women in politics—United States—Biography—
Juvenile literature. [1. Women in politics. 2. Politics,
Practical—Biography] I. Title.
HQ1412.B68   329'.0092'2 [B] [920]   76-5513
ISBN 0-87191-507-3

NEW WOMEN IN POLITICS

4 Bess Myerson

10 Elizabeth Holtzman

14 Dolores Huerta

18 Patsy Mink

26 Barbara Jordan

34 Yvonne Burke

38 Ella Grasso

Bess Myerson

''There she is, Miss America, there she is, your ideal. . . .''

The orchestra swelled into a full crescendo as stately Bess Myerson, Miss America of 1945, began her walk down Atlantic City's famous runway. Thousands of admirers in the audience clapped, cheered, and wept as the new queen smiled out at them across the bright stage lights.

Earlier that evening, Bess — a tall, dark-haired woman from New York City — had stunned the crowd by playing Grieg's *Piano Concerto in A Minor* on the piano and ''Summertime'' on the flute. Now, with the title of ''Miss America,'' Bess Myerson seemed like the leading lady in an all-American ''rags to riches'' success story. She stood at what many Americans regard as the pinnacle of glamour and fame, having spent most of her life on the edge of poverty in the Bronx.

The daughter of Jewish immigrants from Russia, Bess recalls, ''We lived in a one-bedroom apartment . . . where my two sisters and I shared the bedroom and my parents slept in the living room.'' But despite their poverty, Bess's mother managed to find a piano — something, she argued, no family should be without. So on an old battered baby grand, Bess practiced for hours at a time, with her mother shouting out, ''Wrong! That last note was wrong. Play the piece again.''

Bess developed into an accomplished pianist, and after graduation from Hunter College, she decided to get further training in music — *if* she could find the money. It was that same year — 1945 — that the Miss America pageant first offered scholarships to its winning contestants. Bess Myerson could not resist the opportunity and entered the pageant as Miss New York City. ''Frankly, I needed the money,'' she has said, ''and the idea of a week in those big hotels sounded like the limit to me.''

When Bess won the title, she became the first Miss America from New York City, the first Jewish Miss America, and the first Miss America to be a college graduate. She was also enormously popular with the crowd. On that September night in 1945, it seemed certain that with the help of money and fame, the talented Bess Myerson would easily reach her goal of becoming a performing musician.

As it turned out, the Miss America title *did* have a dramatic effect on Bess Myerson's life — but not exactly in ways that she had planned. Bess learned very quickly, for example, that her desire to be a serious, dedicated musician was in conflict with the public's image of ''Miss America.'' Bess recollects, ''After I won the title, I toured vaudeville. I came

6

out in a high-neck gown and played *The Fire Dance* and *Malaguena* on the piano and flute. I could hear the boys up front muttering, 'Where's the bathing suit?' So in the finale I came out wearing a white bathing suit, and the boys would cheer. Toward the end of the tour, I realized they didn't want to hear my music, so I just came out in a bathing suit.''

Trying to be ''the representative of American womanhood'' was, in Bess's words, ''painful — you can't imagine how painful.'' Night after night she would walk through crowded ballrooms and across stages to be peered at, admired, and worshipped. They were difficult hours for a woman who knew that beneath the beauty queen image was a real, living, complex human being who could not even get to know the people who crowded the auditoriums to see her.

Nonetheless, Bess's travels taught her a great deal — about the country she represented and about herself. Bess recalls, ''It was instructive . . . to go to a town below the Mason-Dixon line and to see, actually see, blacks on one side of the street and whites on the other, to be discriminated against myself because of my Jewishness. It was instructive — and it was shocking.''

Seeing these realities of the United States had such a dramatic impact on Bess that she gave up her musical career: ''The Miss America tour convinced me that I wasn't cut out for the insulated life of the musician.'' Instead, she be-

came an extremely successful television personality, starring on "The Big Payoff" and "I've Got a Secret." She also became the familiar float-by-float announcer for the Rose Bowl, Mardi Gras, and Thanksgiving Day parades. It appeared that Bess Myerson had found her permanent niche as a TV star.

Then, in 1969, New York's Mayor John Lindsay appointed Bess Myerson to the post of Commissioner of Consumer Affairs. Many people were startled — how could an ex-beauty queen and TV star possibly hold a government position? Some were convinced that Mayor Lindsay had appointed Bess as mere "window dressing."

But Bess Myerson soon demonstrated the intelligence, energy, and social concern that had always existed behind the image of the beauty queen. Within eight months of taking office, she had persuaded the New York City council to pass some of the strongest consumer protection laws in the country — laws affecting 110 kinds of businesses in the city, from supermarkets to street vendors. What's more, the council gave Bess Myerson the authority to enforce them.

Every day, 80 inspectors from the Consumer Affairs Department (often accompanied by Bess herself) would spread out over New York City. They looked for such legal violations as false advertising, faulty labeling of products, and incorrect weighing and measuring. When the inspectors came across a violation, they issued fines of up to $250. In one year alone, the department found 9,900 violations of the law.

Bess herself was often found in lower-income neighborhoods. "I have always had a great sense of identification with the underprivileged in New York," she has said, and her background has made her extremely sensitive to merchants' attempts to exploit the poor. She spent many hours in supermarkets, looking for such violations as failure to use unit pricing or inaccurate meat-market scales.

But Bess did more than supervise merchants. She encouraged consumers to bring their complaints to her office, which often meant several hundred visits per day. And her staff of 310 made certain that action was taken on each complaint.

At night — dressed in blue jeans and T-shirt — Bess would return to her office to read letters from people who thought they had been swindled.

In her four years as Consumer Affairs Commissioner, Bess Myerson made her department visible, powerful, and accessible to the people of New York City. Worried about reaching the seven million citizens whose lives she affected, Bess began to do two-minute radio spots with tips for consumers. And in 1971, she began a nationally syndicated TV show on consumer advice called, "What Every Woman Wants to Know." There is little doubt that in these areas of her work, Bess was aided considerably by her fame as a former Miss America and TV star.

But her Miss America image haunted her, too. When her department served a subpoena on a supermarket, a newspaper printed photos of both the president of the store and of Bess. The president was pictured in a business suit, and Bess was pictured in a bathing suit! "I think putting labels on people is bad enough," Bess commented, "but putting yesterday's label on somebody is very bad."

Fortunately, Bess's versatility makes putting labels on her nearly impossible. Now that her four-year term as Commissioner of Consumer Affairs is over, Bess is actively engaged in a variety of other activities. She is the author of a guidebook for setting up consumer protection agencies in cities and small towns, she is a columnist for *Redbook* magazine, and she is an adviser for the First National City Bank. And many people are urging her to run for elective political office — perhaps the Senate.

Whatever her specific plans, Bess Myerson is certain to be found in a vital, challenging role — one that positively affects the lives of her fellow Americans. Bess Myerson has remained a famous, respected individual not because of her beauty, but because she utilized the full range of her talents. Bess Myerson wants *not* to be remembered as a beauty queen, but as an instrument of change. For the most vital statistic of all, declares Bess Myerson, ''is the measurement of the human spirit.''

Elizabeth Holtzman

A throng of New Yorkers shuffled impatiently as they stood in line on a congested Brooklyn street. They were waiting to buy tickets to *The Godfather,* and it seemed to many that they'd never get near the box office. Dulled by the summer heat, they listlessly marked their progress by counting the number of cracks they crossed on the hard, sun-baked pavement.

Suddenly out of nowhere appeared a slender, dark-haired woman, energetically moving up and down the row of people. The movie-goers stood firm — guarding their places in line and keeping sharp eyes on the intruder. But this young woman was not interested in the movie — she was interested in *them*. Her bright smile and firm handshake startled the onlookers out of their boredom. ''Hello there, I'm Elizabeth Holtzman,'' she began as she approached individuals in the line. And before they knew it they were comfortably chatting with someone who was running

for the Congress of the United States.

At age 31, Elizabeth Holtzman was a relative newcomer to politics and could not afford expensive campaign advertising or a large staff. So she took the simplest way of making herself known. ''Shoe leather is cheaper than television spots,'' she declared, and the alert young woman in tortoise-shell glasses became a familiar sight at subway stations, bus stops, laundromats, and supermarkets.

Liz Holtzman's opponent in the election was neither young nor new to politics. Eighty-four-year-old Emanuel Celler was a powerful figure who had represented Brooklyn's 16th District for 50 years. In fact, he had first gone to Congress 20 years before Liz Holtzman was even born! Celler was so confident that he described Liz as ''trying to topple the Washington monument with a toothpick,'' and he campaigned with only a handful of appearances and a few fliers mailed out from his office.

For Elizabeth Holtzman, Celler's campaign style was just a symptom of his lack of interest in the people of Brooklyn who had elected him. While serving as an aide to New York's Mayor John Lindsay, she'd had the opportunity to watch Celler close up. Eventually she became so outraged at his apparent disinterest in Brooklyn residents that she decided to run against him.

Using Emanuel Celler's own 1922 slogan, "It's time for a change," Liz Holtzman campaigned with an energy and intensity that startled the residents of Brooklyn. She set up a store-front office in the community and — with the help of family members and college volunteers — talked with voters in their living rooms, on their front steps, and on street corners. With carefully compiled evidence, she was able to point out Emanuel Celler's absence in the community and poor attendance record in Congress. She promised that things

11

would be different if she were to represent them.

Her direct, friendly style appealed to the voters. Elizabeth Holtzman defeated Emanuel Celler in one of the biggest political upsets of the 1972 elections. Called ''Liz the Lion Killer'' by *Time* magazine, Elizabeth Holtzman became the youngest woman ever elected to Congress.

Elizabeth Hotzman continued her aggressive, vigorous style from the day she set foot in Washington. She immediately set out to sponsor legislation dealing with women's rights, low-income housing, and Social Security benefits for the blind and disabled. And in 1973 Elizabeth Holtzman took a dramatic step: she brought suit in Federal District Court challenging President Nixon's bombing of Cambodia without the approval of Congress. The District Court supported her case, and for the first time the war in Cambodia was declared unconstitutional.

Although her activity in Congress has swept Elizabeth Holtzman into national and international affairs, she has never lost her concern for the daily lives of the people of Brooklyn. Keeping her promise that she would be personally available, Liz Holtzman immediately set up an office in Brooklyn where she meets with residents Mondays, Fridays, and Sunday afternoons. It is the first such office in Brooklyn in 50 years and is so busy that it's often referred to as a ''revolving door.''

Since 1973, Elizabeth Holtzman has met with over 4,000 residents, helping them solve a variety of problems — finding a meeting place for a blind Boy Scout troop, rounding up stray dogs, installing traffic lights, or providing litter-baskets for local streets. Whether she is speaking on

12

the floor of Congress or talking to a resident on Flatbush Avenue, Liz Holtzman is vigorously engaged in solving human problems.

For Liz Holtzman, this dedication to both local and national issues means keeping two apartments, two offices, and commuting endlessly between Brooklyn and Washington. It also means little time left over for sailing her boat in Peconic Bay. But Elizabeth Holtzman has found a way of bringing the process of government to the people — something that many politicians neglect to do. The lesson of her victory, says Elizabeth Holtzman, is that ''no political figure, no matter how powerful, can forget about the people he was elected to serve.''

Dolores Huerta

It was five a.m. in California's San Joaquín Valley. The sun rose slowly from behind the ridge of desert hills, outlining them against the hazy pinks and purples of the early morning sky.

In the grape orchards, pick-up trucks dropped empty boxes at the end of each row of vines, sending clouds of dust into the thick, still air. Foremen leaned against their vehicles, watching as crews of Mexican-American and Filipino grape-pickers entered the fields. Brown-skinned, their hands gnarled from years of hard work, they would spend the day in the hot sun, filling the boxes to overflowing with grapes — grapes for wine, grapes for shipment, grapes for dinner tables. And grapes for the profit of the growers.

Suddenly a string of old cars appeared on the road, gradually pulling off onto the shoulder. Doors popped open, and twenty people emerged carrying hats, flags, and bull-horns.

"Well, look what we've got on our hands today," said one foreman to another. "A strike." And he spat angrily into the dirt.

Quickly the strikers positioned themselves near the main crews of workers in the fields. Blood-red flags rose into the air, each one bearing the black, squared-off eagle which was the symbol of the United Farm Workers. Then the picketers began to shout to the workers: "¡HUELGA! ¡VENGANSE, COMPANEROS!" (Strike! Join us, friends!)

Active among the members of the picket line was a slender, dark-haired woman named Dolores Huerta. Her face had the chiseled features of a fine sculpture, but the toughness of someone who has witnessed years of hardship and injustice among her people. As she stood fearlessly beneath a red flag conferring with others about strategy, it became clear that her presence was vital to the strength of the group. "We don't want a *sitting* picket line," she once said. "We want a walking, talking, singing, *shouting* picket line!" And those who had wavered under the heat of the sun revived and took up the call once more: "¡VENGA, VENGA! ¡ALEGRIA!"

By noon, the temperature had reached 100 degrees. Dolores asked a young girl in the field if she might have a glass of water. As the girl brought the glass across the road to Dolores, a foreman came up from behind the girl and kicked the glass from her hand.

The girl began to cry, and soon Dolores was crying with her in outrage at the foreman's cruelty. Before long, thirty farm laborers dropped their tools and walked out of the field

14

to join the strikers. The spirit of the picket line became almost festive, as the solidarity between the poor people in the fields and the poor in the strike group was affirmed.

Cruel incidents are not new to Dolores Huerta, who has been dedicated to helping and organizing farm laborers since 1955. "The workers are treated like animals," she says as her hands tremble with anger. And with her solemn dark eyes fixed upon the listener, she will talk convincingly about the plight of the migrant workers: the hundreds of field hands dying each year after chemical insecticides have been sprayed on them, the total yearly incomes of $1500, the ramshackle housing, and the poor nutrition. Because migrant workers are not covered by federal labor laws, Dolores points out that they have not been protected with child labor regulations, minimum wages, or unemployment benefits. It was in response to these conditions that the organization of the United Farm Workers was formed. Dolores Huerta is now First Vice-President of the organization.

But for Dolores Huerta, mother of seven children, working as the captain of picket lines is only one of many jobs. She can be found in New York, organizing urban grocers and consumers to boycott produce shipped by companies which will not negotiate for better working conditions. Or she can be found speaking to groups of just about any size or composition that want to hear about the work of the United Farm organization. And she can be found across the table from the powerful wine growers. Unintimidated by their power, wealth, or status, she debates fine points of logic and law.

Dolores is deeply committed to organizing the people of the fields — the poor, illiterate, and forgotten — putting into their hands some of the power to affect their own lives. And for Dolores Huerta that means working in the fields, on the picket lines, in their homes, in their churches — wherever the vital bonds among people can be strengthened and unified. She has said, "I kind of think of organizing as sacred work . . . it's a big responsibility, you know getting people's hopes up, and then if you abandon them . . . well, you've ruined their aspirations, and you've spoiled the faith they have to have in anybody else who tries to help them."

16

A POEM OF THE MEXICAN FARM WORKER
My father . . .
could not write
very many words
But when he brought in
his crop
in the heat of a summer afternoon
he created
a poem . . . from the earth.
                Anonymous

Patsy Mink

"THINK MINK!" That's what many Hawaiians were saying in 1964 — on T-shirts, bumper stickers, and yard signs. The reason? Patsy Takemoto Mink was seeking election to the United States House of Representatives. She hoped to become the first woman from the 50th state to be a member of Congress.

After a whirlwind campaign of island-hopping, speeches, and often five or six coffee-hours in one evening, Patsy Mink achieved her goal on election day. And the new congresswoman was hailed as the most important woman in Hawaiian politics since Queen Liliuokalani was dethroned in 1893.

Patsy Mink celebrated her victory by painting in the missing eye on a *daruma* doll — a papier maché doll whose eyes, by Japanese tradition, are painted in only after one's secret wishes come true. "I painted one eye in after the primary," Patsy recounts, "the other when I was elected to Congress. Nobody at headquarters knew what the doll was there for.

It's really a very private thing — like when you see a falling star, you don't tell everyone what you're wishing."

Although Patsy Mink had been president of the student body at Maui High School, politics had not figured in her original career plans. Impressed by her family's physician, Patsy enrolled in premedicine at the University of Hawaii. But after graduating with a degree in zoology and chemistry, she decided that a law career would give her more independence.

Patsy applied to the University of Chicago Law School and was accepted — by accident. "A quota for foreigners existed," recalls Patsy, "and some idiot there thought Hawaii was a foreign country, so I was accepted."

In the early 1950's, Patsy returned to Hawaii with her law degree, as well as a husband and a new baby daughter. "My ambition was simply to be a practicing attorney — one of the best," Patsy recalls of that period.

18

19

But none of the law firms she applied to would hire her. ''Stay home and take care of your child,'' they told her. So Patsy opened up an office of her own, renting the space for $50 a month. While she waited for clients Patsy became active in community affairs and in the Democratic Party. She organized the Young Democrats of Oahu, and in 1956 became the first Territorial president of the Hawaii Young Democrats.

Eventually, after spending a great deal of time helping others get elected to public office, Patsy Mink decided to give it a try herself. She filed for a seat in the legislature. In making this decision, Patsy received very little encouragement from her parents. ''Like most natives, they are quiet and retiring, and therefore were fearful of the publicity — for themselves and for me.'' But after Patsy won the 1956 election to the Territorial House, they were able, she states, ''to understand that I no longer needed to be protected from anything.''

A major source of support for Patsy Mink's political career has been her husband John, who served as her campaign manager when she sought (and won) election to the U.S. House of Representatives in 1964. According to Patsy Mink, this teamwork between husband and wife is essential: ''You rarely find a successful man in politics who doesn't have the active, total support of his wife. Likewise, a woman should have the support of her husband before seeking public office.'' Support, however, does not mean instant agreement. John Mink views himself as one of Patsy's advisers: ''We discuss the issues, take positions, have differences of opinion, and eventually come to some sort of consensus. The final decision in any vote in Congress, though, is Patsy's.''

When Patsy Mink arrived in Washing-

21

ton in 1964, her colleagues soon learned that beneath her petite, pretty image was a sharp-witted, articulate woman who held tenacious views on many issues.

Patsy came to Congress at the peak of United States involvement in the war in Vietnam — an involvement she called an example of United States racism. It encouraged, she claimed, the killing of Asians by other Asians. Americans needed to stop pretending, argued Patsy Mink, that Western European culture was the only guide for human destiny: ''We need to know that there has been culture in Asia, and science and art, going back for thousands of years. The Caucasian race alone cannot lay claim to all the triumphs of human ingenuity. . . . Oriental life is no less valuable than European life.'' Her position on the war cost her many votes in her home district (where military installations support the economy). Still, Patsy consistently spoke out against the war and argued for amnesty for those Americans who refused to serve in the Army.

Patsy Mink's concern for human rights extends also to equal opportunities for women. ''Patsy was a liberated woman long before the movement had a name,'' one Democrat has observed. And it is true that Patsy Mink has been ahead of her time with respect to women's rights. As long ago as 1958, Patsy was instrumental in Hawaii's passage of an Equal Pay for Equal Work law. The Federal law was not passed until 1963.

Patsy Mink has become noted for her efforts to eliminate discrimination against women in all aspects of American life. Each year, her office receives about 500 cases of reported sex discrimination, and Patsy is frequently able to resolve the problems. Once she found out, for example, that women were not permitted to be postal inspectors. Patsy complained instantly to the Postmaster General, and

23

within two weeks the Post Office Department was accepting applications from women.

Discrimination against women begins at an early age, however, when young girls and boys are taught that boys become the doctors, scientists, and engineers, while girls fill the roles of secretaries, nurses, and waitresses. The result is that girls believe that they have very few choices when planning their careers. To help counteract this problem, Patsy Mink wrote a piece of landmark legislation called the "Women's Educational Equity Act Bill." It appropriates funds so that teachers learn new and better ways of working with boys and girls to expand their life's choices, so that up-to-date books

and materials can be produced, and so that centers are developed which help women return to work after their children are grown.

Because of her dedication to equal rights, in 1972 a group of people from Oregon invited Patsy Mink to enter the Presidential primary in that state. Patsy accepted the invitation, saying, "Without a female contending for the Presidency, the concept of *absolute equality* will continue to be placed on the back-burner as warmed-over lip service."

Although Patsy received only 2% of the vote in the primary, the experience convinced her that "there'll be a woman Vice President sooner than might otherwise have been the case." And Patsy

Mink considers it vital that women be in top level government positions, working cooperatively with men. ''Women are capable of making tough decisions,'' she declares, and they also have a great deal of ''compassion, creativity, sensitivity and plain common sense. They could make tremendous contributions in fields that naturally interest them . . . the education of their children, the health of their families, air and water pollution, their husbands, jobs. Aren't these all prime concerns of government?''

When Patsy Mink came to Washington over a decade ago, she said she brought to Congress ''a Hawaiian background of tolerance and quality that contribute a great deal to better understand-ing between races.'' Over the years, she has extended her concern for equality to include any people who are oppressed, disenfranchised, and stigmatized. The basis of Patsy Mink's politics is *humanism* — the belief that people are more important than power, profit, and the bureaucracy. For many Americans this political philosophy holds out a bit of hope for the governmental process following the disillusioning days of Watergate and illegal campaign financing. Patsy Mink believes this hope is essential to restoring integrity to American life: ''Only a small flame is needed,'' she says, ''to ignite the smouldering masses of people who despair . . . but who want to believe again.''

25

Barbara Jordan

"It can't be possible," thought Barbara Jordan as she lifted an armload of heavy black books into her car. "How can anyone even think about removing the President of the United States from office?"

But there on the seat of her car sat the silent testimony to the possibility — huge volumes containing the case against President Richard M. Nixon.

Barbara sank into the driver's seat, wiping beads of moisture from her forehead. She was weary from the long walk to the parking lot and burdened by the weight of the task before her. Soon, she and the other members of the House Judiciary Committee would make a recommendation to the House regarding the impeachment of President Richard Nixon. The assignment was an awesome beginning to Barbara Jordan's first term in the U.S. House of Representatives.

As she maneuvered her car through Washington's late afternoon traffic, Barbara's face bore a continual frown. "The President of the United States is one of the most respected people in the world," she mused. "Only once before in the history of this country has impeachment been considered . . . how can I arrive at a fair decision?"

26

When she spotted the National Archives building, Barbara pulled into the first vacant parking space, got out, and locked the car. Dressed in a tailored suit, Barbara wore no jewelry or make-up — as if those pre-occupations were too frivolous for such momentous days in history. Once inside the building, Barbara wound her way flawlessly through a maze of corridors — as if drawn like a magnet to a powerful source.

And suddenly there it was. The Constitution of the United States. Safe in its airtight glass case. Safe from the hands of reckless tourists and malicious vandals. Barbara paused to catch her breath, then stood in line amid the sightseers until she could get a better view. Finally, her serious brown eyes were able to study the famous words of the Preamble:

WE, THE PEOPLE OF THE UNITED STATES, IN ORDER TO FORM A MORE PERFECT UNION, ESTABLISH JUSTICE, INSURE DOMESTIC TRANQUILITY . . .

The words pressed heavily upon her mind: *we, people, union, justice, tranquility.* These were the ideas, she realized, which were at the core of the decision ahead of her. In judging the President, she would return to the principles upon which the country was founded 200 years earlier — principles which rose above the power of any single human being.

With a clearer vision of the work ahead of her, Barbara headed home. That night, as she had for many weeks, she pored over the contents of the heavy black books — sitting alone into the still hours of the morning, thinking, making notes, and searching within herself. ''The evidence against the President is mounting,'' she thought to herself, shaking her head solemnly. These were grim hours for a woman with such belief in her country that she always saluted the flag and got goose bumps at the sound of the National Anthem.

But they weren't the first difficult times in the political life of Barbara Jordan. She had first run for office in 1962, borrowing every cent of the $500 filing fee. Recalling her attempt to win a seat in the Texas House of Representatives, she says, ''I felt that if politicians were believable . . . the people would overlook race, sex and poverty — and elect me. They did not.'' It wasn't easy to be black and female and to come out a winner.

After losing again in 1964, Barbara became discouraged. She even considered moving to another section of the country where a black woman might stand a better chance of being elected. But she changed her mind: ''I didn't *want* to do this. I am a Texan; my roots are in Texas. To leave would be a cop-out. So I stayed.''

Barbara's commitment and determination paid off. In 1966, she won a seat in the Texas State Senate, becoming the first black elected since 1883. But the struggle was not over. Barbara realized that the leadership of the Senate was white, conservative, and male. Barbara knew that she would have to win her colleagues' respect in order to effectively represent the people who had voted for her. And those voters had a lot at stake in Barbara Jordan. They were largely black, Chicano, and poor white — people who had traditionally been left out of the political process.

So Barbara Jordan began by identifying the most powerful members of the Senate. By carefully observing them, she discovered the methods they used to be effective and influential legislators. Then she decided to try those methods herself and was quickly able to use the fine points of parliamentary procedure to her advantage. Soon Barbara had gained the respect of even the most conservative legislators for her keen mind, her forthrightness, and her superb handling of issues on the floor of the Senate. At the end of her first term, her fellow senators voted her the outstanding freshman member. And in 1972, Barbara Jordan achieved an even higher honor — she was elected to the United States House of Representatives, winning an impressive 81% of the vote. Her following had broadened considerably: ''Lots of white people voted for me,'' she said, ''and it was because they felt their interest would be included.'' The woman who had needed to borrow the filing fee for her first election had clearly and powerfully broken into national government.

29

Now, in her role as congresswoman, she faced the coming vote on the impeachment of President Nixon. Day after day, she sat through the debates in a huge leather chair that failed to dwarf her handsome, imposing figure. Much of the time she was quiet and motionless — leaning back with her head tipped slightly to one side as she listened and concentrated. And when Barbara Jordan decided to speak out, everyone listened.

"The chair recognizes the gentlelady from Texas," rasped Peter Rodino, head of the committee, during one of the sessions. Barbara Jordan leaned slowly and deliberately toward the microphone. The room fell silent. She was about to speak as a black woman who had some special things to say about her nation's history:

" 'We, the people' — it is a very eloquent beginning. But when the Constitution of the United States was completed on the 17th of September in 1787, I was not included in that 'We, the people.' I felt for many years that somehow George Washington and Alexander Hamilton just

31

32

left me out by mistake. But through the process of amend-
ment, interpretation, and court decision, I have finally been
included in 'We, the people. . . .' "

　　Barbara Jordan knew that ultimately it had been the
Constitution which had ensured a place for her — and for
others — in America's political processes. And there was
more work to be done. She was not about to let the behavior
of a President put that document in jeopardy:

　　"My faith in the Constitution is whole, it is complete, it
is total," she concluded. "I am not going to sit here and be
an idle spectator to the diminution, the subversion, the de-
struction of the Constitution."

　　And so it was that Barbara Jordan became one of the
Committee members to cast a formal vote for the impeachment of Richard M. Nixon. She knew that the piece of paper
called the Constitution was safe in an airtight case in the
National Archives. But she also knew that the safety of its
principles depended upon the behavior of its citizens and of
the powerful people who govern them.

　　"We, the people" is a special phrase for Barbara Jordan, and it has given her a special dream for America; "I
want to see the day when we — everybody — can feel like
we belong here, that this country has to survive because we
have to survive, that our future is bound up in the future of the
nation."

Yvonne Burke

"Do you know the way to San José? I've been away so long, I may go wrong and lose my way. . . ."

Heads turned all along busy Pennsylvania Avenue as Dionne Warwick's familiar tones floated out the windows of a white Lincoln Continental. Driving the car was a strikingly beautiful woman who was tapping out the rhythm of the song on the steering wheel. Diamond pendant earrings swung gently against her neck as her head moved in time to the music.

"Who's that — some movie star?" a man on the street asked his companion.

"Don't you recognize her? That's Yvonne Brathwaite Burke — a member of Congress."

"You've gotta be kidding. With those looks, she could be in Hollywood!"

That's what many people in Washington say about vivacious Yvonne Brathwaite Burke, the first black woman from California elected to the U.S. House of Representatives. And in truth, Yvonne Burke *has* been in Hollywood. The first times were in her childhood, when she would accompany her father, an MGM janitor, to picket lines during labor disputes. And later, while a student at the University of California in Los Angeles, Yvonne starred in several films and theatre productions. These experiences, however, did not draw her toward the fame and glitter of Hollywood stardom but rather toward a career in law and politics. For what she remembers most about Hollywood are the injustices she witnessed toward blacks and other minorities.

Today, Yvonne Burke is without doubt one of the most beautiful members of Congress. She is also well-known for her tough, determined stands on child care, housing, and education — areas where human rights are often at stake. The black congresswoman's sensitivity to these

34

issues comes in part from over forty years of facing discrimination in her own life.

When Yvonne started school, the principal decided that Yvonne needed more competition. So her parents transferred their exceptionally bright daughter to a school connected with the University of Southern California. As it turned out, Yvonne was the only black student, and she faced many incidents of harassment from whites. But Yvonne responded to the situation with calm and persistence — traits which came to dominate her style. By the time she was in high school, the confident young woman had become vice-president of the student body.

But prejudice struck again when Yvonne was a law student at the University of Southern California. A women's society on the campus would not let blacks or Jews join. Yvonne's response? She and two Jewish girls began a chapter of a different sorority!

And a few years later when Yvonne applied for an apartment in Sacramento, a landlady turned her down because she was black. Some of her friends urged her to confront the landlady, while others told her to forget about it. Yvonne did neither. After careful thought, she filed a complaint with the Fair Employment Practices Commission. Yvonne got the apartment, and her friends got a sample of her style: no pickets, no foot-stomping, no shrill voice. But quiet action that gets results.

Yvonne continues in Congress today with her practical, no-nonsense approach to issues. She works diligently for equal opportunities for women in all areas of society. And that includes politics, where women have been extremely underrepresented. She encourages women to be lobbyists and members of legislative staffs — two key positions of political impact.

Yvonne Burke is hopeful that society will expand its vision of women and racial minorities in the next generation. Her optimism became apparent in a lighthearted incident following the birth of her daughter in 1973. When someone asked if little Autumn Roxanne would grow up to be a congresswoman like her mother, Yvonne responded, ''No. She's going to be President.''

Ella Grasso

38

It's seven o'clock on a sleepy Saturday morning in Hartford, Connecticut. But the shops on the South Side are already beginning to open up, and conversations in Portuguese, Italian, and French punctuate the hazy morning air. Store owners are busy sweeping, pulling back awnings, and setting out their merchandise.

Walking along the street, stopping to chat with almost everyone she sees, is a short, stocky woman with close-cropped brown hair. From time to time she playfully captures one of the kids dodging the delivery trucks, then returns to sampling the rolls from the bakeries and the sausages from the meats shops. She expresses her enthusiasm to the shop owners in their native languages. ''Che buono!'' she tells the Italian butcher. ''Magnifique'' is her judgment of the French baker's sweet roll.

But her real hunger seems to be for news. She wants to know how they are doing with the rising prices of ingredients, about the new baby in the family, about the son away in the army. She gestures vigorously as she comments on what they tell her, widening her brown eyes at some of their news.

The woman is Ella Grasso, the Governor of Connecticut. Her energy for mingling with the people of her state seems boundless. ''There is a real relationship between government and what happens to people in their everyday lives,'' she has said. And Ella Grasso is a woman who acts on that belief.

After several hours on the South Side, she journeys to the North Side of the city to talk with residents of largely Irish and black neighborhoods. Her brown eyes are riveted on the faces of the people as she absorbs the details that will affect the decisions in the governor's office. A familiar visitor to the streets of the North Side, Ella Grasso is trusted with the facts of citizens' lives — with their fear that the factories will lay off more people, with a rising crime rate, with run-down housing. Ella promises to return the next week to visit local factories and to send a housing inspector to talk to landlords.

From the neighborhoods of Hartford, Ella Grasso continued on that day to a meeting of Young Democrats, a party for senior citizens, a dinner given by an association for retarded children, and a late-night party for Portuguese veterans.

"Aren't you getting tired?" an aide finally asked her.

Ella laughed. "Actually I am. I went to a party last night and danced the tarantella all evening," she confessed. As the aide looked down at her feet, he saw that Ella had worn a pair of moccasins in anticipation of the long day on the streets.

For Ella Grasso, a whirlwind schedule is nothing unusual. It's been her style for 22 years of political life. A plain woman who wears no make-up, simple clothing, and a no-nonsense hair style, Ella shuns the "glamorous" side of politics. It's the *people* she's interested in.

At big political events she never stays long at the table, even when she is the guest of honor. Instead, she is off mingling in the crowd, firmly shaking hands, making introductions, hugging old friends, and welcoming newcomers. In politics it's often called the "down-home" style. It's a style that's natural for Ella, and it seems to please the voters. Ella Grasso hasn't lost an election in over 20 years. One observer has said, "Everyone knows Ella, from one end of the state to the other. They know she's smart and they know they can trust her."

41

42

The story of Ella Grasso's political life is one of ever-widening circles of influence and fame. Yet she has never lost her sense of rootedness in her home community. This connection with people has caused many people to say that she is one of the most popular and approachable women in politics today.

Ella's political career began at the grass roots level in 1943 when she joined the local League of Women Voters. This experience made her look to bigger goals, and in 1952 she won a seat in the Connecticut House of Representatives.

When she went off to her new job, she was able to leave her children, 4-year-old Susane and 18-month-old Jim, with her Italian mother. Ella says, ''I was part of an extended family. . . . My parents lived across the street, the street was short, and everyone was there before I was born. I had other family in the neighborhood, too.'' It was not only Ella's mother who played a role in her success. Her father once had worked fourteen hours a day in a bakery so that Ella could get an education, and he often accompanied Ella when she gave campaign speeches. His grateful daughter never failed to introduce him from the podium.

After Ella had arrived at the Connecticut House of Representatives, she worried that she would never get ahead in politics — not because she wasn't knowledgeable, but because the men did their conferring in the rest room, and Ella couldn't join in! But that proved to be no handicap. She was re-elected two years later.

Next Ella Grasso took on an even more powerful and difficult job — as Connecticut's Secretary of State. In that position, which she held for twelve years, she worked especially hard in the areas of civil rights, day care, and mental hospital reform. Kathy Johnson, a young woman who worked for Ella during that period, recalls, "She ran an extremely tight ship. When you were in the office there was no play time. There was never any political campaigning conducted during office hours. She's always been super honest, Mrs. Clean."

From her state position, it seemed that the only direction was up — to national politics. Ella Grasso decided to run for Congress. Her campaign style was typical for the friendly, gracious woman: very few formal speeches or TV appearances, but lots of visits to neighborhoods, factories, and homes to talk to people directly. And in 1971 she was elected to the Congress of the United States.

Once in Washington, she continued her habit of maintaining direct contact with the people she represented. Her small, cramped office was extremely informal and nearly overrun with a constant stream of visitors. It came to be called the "people's lobby." And amid the hustle and bustle of drafting bills, writing speeches, and answering letters, Ella took time personally to hear the problems and opinions of countless citizens.

For those who could not come to see her personally, she installed a toll-free "Ella-Phone." Twenty-four hours a day, anyone in the Connecticut district she served could reach Ella or one of her staff. She said, "It's my way of bringing government closer to the people and the people closer to government."

In 1974, Ella decided to run for Governor of Connecticut. No one who knew Ella was surprised that she would again want to take a state office. Her years in Congress had been

44

successful politically, but they had meant separation from her family and her beloved community. "I found my four years in Washington most instructive," she has said. "But I would have been happier if they had moved the capital to Hartford."

Ella won the election by 200,000 votes, becoming the nation's first woman governor in her own right. (A few other women have served as governor, but only in the footsteps of their husbands or as their widows.) In her new role Ella again set up an office that was accessible to the people. For one thing, she does not want the Governor's Mansion to be considered a "home" only for her. She wants it to be used by the people of Connecticut. "It's a smashing place to hold a meeting or reception," she declares, pushing her half-glasses from the tip of her nose to the top of her head. "I intend to begin a series of little parties for senior citizens as soon as the weather changes."

Happily for Ella, she is able to spend some time at her spacious, barn-styled home in Windsor Locks, the community where she was born and grew up. Often she sits near two telephones, with one ringing as she talks on the other — forever staying in touch with her people.

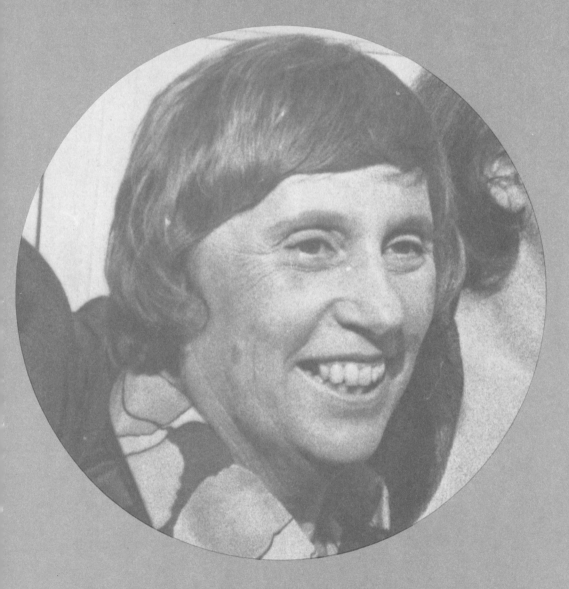

"When she's talking to you, you think you're the most wonderful person in the world," one Connecticut woman has commented. The amazing thing is that Ella Grasso has kept this personable quality through 22 years of political success and national fame. But the people of Windsor Locks never expected anything else. To them she's still just "Ella."

47